ENGLISH PHRASAL VERBS BOOK 3

3 WORDS A DAY

KEITH S. FOLSE

KELLY SIPPELL

WAYZGOOSE PRESS

English Phrasal Verbs Book 3. 3 Words a Day

Keith S. Folse, Ph.D., Kelly Sippell

Copyright © 2024 Keith S. Folse

Published by Wayzgoose Press

Edited by Dorothy Zemach and Bella Graham

Cover by GetCovers.com

ISBN: 978-1-961953-11-6

All rights reserved.

No part of this book may be reproduced in any form or by any electronic or mechanical means, including information storage and retrieval systems, without written permission from the author, except for the use of brief quotations in a book review.

Legal Disclaimer: All company names and websites mentioned in this book are trademarks or copyrights of their respective owners. The author is not affiliated with them in any way and does not endorse them or their ideas.

CONTENTS

List of Verbs   v
Introduction   ix

Lesson 1   1
cut off; pull up; turn back

Lesson 2   12
clean up; set out; shut down

Lesson 3   22
slow down; turn over; wind up

Lesson 4   31
lay out; take back; turn up

Lesson 5   41
go over; hold on; line up

Lesson 6   51
go through; hang up; pay off

Lesson 7   62
break up; hold out; pull back

Lesson 8   72
bring out; build up; hang on

Lesson 9   82
get down; put on; throw out

Lesson 10   92
come over; hang out; move in

About the Publisher   101

LIST OF VERBS

PHRASAL VERBS IN BOOK 3 (BY LESSON)

Lesson 1: cut off; pull up; turn back

Lesson 2: clean up; set out; shut down

Lesson 3: slow down; turn over; wind up

Lesson 4: lay out; take back; turn up

Lesson 5: go over; hold on; line up

Lesson 6: go through; hang up; pay off

Lesson 7: break up; hold out; pull back

Lesson 8: bring out; build up; hang on

Lesson 9: get down; put on; throw out

Lesson 10: come over; hang out; move in

PHRASAL VERBS IN BOOK 3 (ALPHABETICAL)

Lesson numbers in parentheses represent the first use of a phrasal verb: (7)

Lesson numbers in brackets represent a recycled phrasal verb: [10]

break up (7)

bring out (8) [10]

build up (8)

clean up (2) [4, 9]

come over (10)

cut off (1) [2, 5, 7]

get down (9)

go over (5) [6]

go through (6) [7, 10]

hang on (8) [9]

hang out (10)

hang up (6) [10]

hold on (5)

hold out (7)

lay out (4) [6]

line up (5) [6]

move in (10)

pay off (6) [7]

pull back (7)

pull up (1) [2, 3]

put on (9)

set out (2) [4]

shut down (2) [3]

slow down (3) [4]

take back (4)

throw out (9)

turn back (1) [3]

turn over (3) [5]

turn up (4) [5, 7, 10]

wind up (3) [4, 5, 10]

INTRODUCTION

Phrasal verbs are one of the most difficult parts of English. They cause headaches for English learners no matter what your first language is. This book will help you with the phrasal verbs that are most frequent in spoken English.

To function well in a new language, you need vocabulary—and lots of it! Some studies say you can do simple things with just 1,000 words, but you can't really speak any language with just 1,000 words. Other experts have said you need 5,000 words, and some recent studies now say you need 10,000 (or even more!) words to speak your new language well. The more vocabulary you have in a new language, the better your speaking and listening will be.

A **phrasal verb** is one type of vocabulary. It consists of a verb and a preposition. The verb is usually a very simple short word like *get, make,* or *take*. The most common prepositions in phrasal verbs (in order of frequency) include *out, in, up, down, on, off, back,* and *over* (Gardner and Davies, 2007).

The problem for English learners is that these two words together have **a new meaning that is not the same as the meaning of just the verb or the meaning of just the preposition.** If you know the meaning of the verb and the meaning of the preposition, it does not mean you know the meaning of the phrasal verb. The meanings are often very different.

For example, let's look at the phrasal verb *call off*. *Call* mostly means to contact someone on the phone, and *off* is the opposite of *on*. But *call off* means *cancel* and has no connection to a phone: *The coach called off the game*. Other examples include *figure out, go on,* and *show up*.

Learning phrasal verbs is very difficult. English has hundreds of phrasal verbs, and each phrasal verb can have several meanings. In fact, frequently used phrasal verbs can have more than five different meanings.

WHY ARE THE 150 PHRASAL VERBS IN THESE BOOKS IMPORTANT?

You can easily find a list of phrasal verbs on the internet, but those are just lists taken from big dictionaries. Many of those phrasal verbs are not so common, which makes them a waste of your time, and your time is important.

In these five books about phrasal verbs, you will practice the 150 most frequently used phrasal verbs in English. This list is the result of an extensive computer analysis of a large collection of approximately 130 million words of spoken English (PHaVE List: Garnier and Schmitt, 2015).

Sometimes one phrasal verb can have five or more meanings, so what should you learn first? You should learn the most common meanings, so the books in this series teach only the top meanings of each phrasal verb based on important information from a very detailed study by Liu and Myers (2020). The meanings are listed **in order of frequency**, so the first meaning is more frequently used than the second meaning, etc. (A few changes from the original list have been made for better learning.)

In sum, these books teach the most common phrasal verbs with the most common meanings in spoken English. Information about the 150 verbs chosen for these books comes from these sources:

Adolphs, Svenja, and Dawn Knight. "Building a spoken corpus." *The Routledge handbook of corpus linguistics* (2010): 38–52.

Davies, Mark. *The corpus of contemporary American English (COCA)*. (2008-): available online at https://www.english-corpora.org/coca/.

Gardner, Dee, and Mark Davies. "Pointing out frequent phrasal verbs: A corpus-based analysis." *TESOL Quarterly* 41.2 (2007): 339–359.

Garnier, Mélodie, and Norbert Schmitt. "The PHaVE List: A pedagogical list of phrasal verbs and their most frequent meaning senses." *Language Teaching Research* 19.6 (2015): 645–666.

Garnier, Mélodie, and Norbert Schmitt. "Picking up polysemous phrasal verbs: How many do learners know and what facilitates this knowledge?" *System* 59 (2016): 29–44.

Liu, Dilin. "The most frequently used English phrasal verbs in American and British English: A multicorpus examination." *TESOL Quarterly* 45.4 (2011): 661–688.

Liu, Dilin, and Daniel Myers. "The most-common phrasal verbs with their key meanings for spoken and academic written English: A corpus analysis." *Language Teaching Research* 24.3 (2020): 403–424.

HOW ARE THESE BOOKS ORGANIZED?

There are five books. The phrasal verbs in Book 1 are more common than those in Book 2, etc., so you should start with Book 1 and continue through the books in order: 2, 3, 4, 5. The order is based on an analysis of millions of words of real English. The phrasal verbs in Book 3 are more advanced and help you further improve your English speaking and listening.

Each book has 10 lessons. Each lesson has 3 phrasal verbs. That lesson will focus on those 3 phrasal verbs, but it will also review some of the phrasal verbs from earlier lessons, so you should also do the lessons in order.

Each lesson has these **6 practice activities**:

- **Activity 1**: CONVERSATION PRACTICE
- **Activity 2**: LEARNING NEW PHRASAL VERBS
- **Activity 3**: PRACTICING IMPORTANT PHRASES

- **Activity 4**: USING CORRECT PREPOSITIONS
- **Activity 5**: VERBS IN CONTEXT
- **Activity 6**: ONLINE PRACTICE (with a link allowing for 5 different kinds of online practice, including one for instruction)

PRACTICAL ADVICE FOR LEARNING VOCABULARY

You need a lot of vocabulary, and no one can learn this vocabulary for you. A good teacher and a good book can help, but in the end, it's all up to you.

To get more vocabulary, you need to read things in English that interest you. You need to practice speaking in English. You should try to find a conversation partner who can help you practice your lessons of three English phrasal verbs.

Keep a vocabulary notebook, either a traditional paper notebook or an electronic notebook. Every time you see a new English word, write it down. Ask yourself, "Is this word important for me in my English?" If the answer is yes, then ask, "How is this word used?" If the answer is no, then skip it and keep looking for another word.

To remember a new word, look at it carefully. Is there anything different or special about the word that can help you remember it? Is the spelling unusual or new to you? Is the word really long? Does it have any double letters?

Examples:

- VALLEY: You can remember the word *valley* because it begins with the letter V and a valley is shaped like the letter V.
- ENVELOPE: You can remember the word *envelope* because it starts with *e* and ends with *e*, and not many words in English start and end with the letter *e*.
- MUSTARD: A personal example is the word *mustard*. I like mustard a lot, so I know I need that word when I order a sandwich at a restaurant. If I don't know this word, then I should look for that word in a dictionary and then think of something to help me remember it. To do this well, I am going to imagine a big yellow **M** on top of my sandwich, representing mustard. Whenever you find a new word, try to find something that makes that word different or special to you personally.
- DOZEN: Every time you see a new word that you think is useful for your English purposes, you should stop and make a short example in your head. If the word is *dozen*, then say to yourself, "one dozen eggs, one dozen pencils, one dozen sandwiches." It's okay to practice English with yourself in your own head. This is in fact very good practice. Use the new word and then talk to yourself (silently). It can be something as simple as "I would like some mustard, please." Yes, practice English with yourself by making a short example with each new word.

10 SUGGESTIONS FOR USING THIS BOOK

1. Open the book! Do the lessons! Many students buy a new book but do not complete the book. This book has only 10 lessons, and each lesson is short. Make time to read the book.
2. Do all the exercises. Even if an exercise seems easy, do it. The more times your brain "touches" each phrasal verb, the better your English vocabulary will become.
3. Each lesson teaches you only 3 phrasal verbs, but these verbs can have several meanings. In fact, some have two meanings, but others have five. Everyone learns differently. Some people can do one lesson in one day, but most people will need a few days with each lesson, so work hard and try to learn these very common, very useful phrasal verbs.
4. When you learn a new phrasal verb, try to learn a very short phrase with the verb. For example, when you learn FIND OUT, you should learn FIND OUT THE ANSWER or FIND OUT HER PHONE NUMBER. When you learn SET UP, you should try to remember SET UP AN APPOINTMENT or SET UP A MEETING.
5. Translations are very good when you first learn a new phrasal verb, but a translation is not your final goal. Your goal is to understand and use the phrasal verb. After you have a clear translation, then make sure you do Step 4: Learn a short phrase with the verb.
6. Every time you see a new phrasal verb, immediately try to make a personal example in your head. For example, when you learn PICK UP, ask yourself,

"How can I make an example with PICK UP about my life now?" Maybe you will say, "I need to PICK UP my friend at the airport tonight" or "Please PICK UP the baby." Say this example in your head. Write it down. It is much better if you practice your new phrasal verb in your head before you try to use it in real conversation.

7. Try to use your new vocabulary in your conversations in English. If you have a conversation partner, share your list of 3 phrasal verbs from your lesson and tell your partner that the goal is to use these 3 phrasal verbs as much as possible in your conversation.
8. Do not worry about mistakes. Remember: Practice makes perfect, so practice, practice, practice!
9. This book has many examples and exercises for each phrasal verb, but some people can remember vocabulary better if they can watch a lesson about it from a teacher. One good place to find free and easy-to-access lessons about phrasal verbs is YouTube. For example, if your new phrasal verb is *call off*, just search for "phrasal verb call off" and you will find many short lessons. Some videos are better than others, so if you find a teacher you like, then for the second phrasal verb, see if that same teacher also has a YouTube video lesson about other phrasal verbs.
10. Finally, try to use the phrasal verbs you learned in Book 1 and Book 2. The more you practice all of these verbs, the better your English will be.

Good luck learning lots of English vocabulary!

Keith S. Folse and Kelly Sippell

LESSON 1
CUT OFF; PULL UP; TURN BACK

ACTIVITY 1: CONVERSATION PRACTICE

Two friends are talking about a time change.

Read this conversation. Think about the meanings of the **3 new bold verbs**. Then answer the comprehension questions.

Fatimah: Hi, Paul. How's it going?
Paul: Hi, Fatimah. Oh, it's been a long week. I'm really looking forward to that extra hour of sleep tomorrow night.
Fatimah: An extra hour of sleep?
Paul: Yes, have you forgotten? It's the first weekend in November, so this is the weekend that we **turn back** the clocks one hour and end Daylight Saving Time.
Fatimah: Oh, that's right. This is new to me. Where I grew up, we didn't change our clocks.
Paul: Really? I thought everyone in the US **turned back** their clocks one hour this time of year.
Fatimah: Well, I grew up in Saudi Arabia, where we never change the time. But I have heard that in the US, there are two states—Arizona and Hawaii, I think—that don't change, and, of course, most other countries don't either.
Paul: That's interesting.
Fatimah: In fact, I read that some US states have recently passed laws to stop changing the time twice a year. They say it's a very old law and doesn't make sense anymore.
Paul: What do you mean?
Fatimah: These states want Daylight Saving Time to be permanent, so there would be no turning clocks forward in the spring or **turning** clocks **back** in the fall. In fact, around 20 states have already passed laws to do this.

Paul: But how would that work if some places change time and others don't?

Fatimah: I don't know. I guess there would have to be a national law. All 50 states have to agree to stop **turning** the clocks **back** in the fall and ahead in the spring. Right now, there are still too many states that don't want the law to change.

Paul: Oh. Well, I really like getting one extra hour of sleep in the fall, so I'd be sad to see it end.

Fatimah: Right, but then you wouldn't have to lose an hour of sleep in the spring, when you go back to Daylight Saving Time.

Paul: True. Hey, when does that happen exactly?

Fatimah: Let me **pull up** my calendar app. It looks like it's usually the second weekend in March.

Paul: Well, I'm just going to enjoy the extra hour of sleep this weekend and not think about March yet.

Fatimah: Hey, I'm sorry to have to **cut** you **off,** but I'm going to be late for my next meeting.

Paul: No problem. See you later.

1. What is Paul happy about?

    a. He likes the weather at this time of year.
    b. He likes watching TV on weekends.
    c. He likes getting an extra hour of sleep one night in the fall.

2. When is this conversation taking place?

   a. It is probably November.
   b. It is probably March.
   c. It is probably September.

3. Where did Fatimah grow up?

   a. Arizona
   b. Saudi Arabia
   c. We don't know from this conversation.

4. Based on this conversation, do Canada and Mexico also have Daylight Saving Time?

   a. Yes, both countries have Daylight Saving Time.
   b. Mexico has Daylight Saving Time, but Canada does not.
   c. We don't know from this conversation.

5. Why have some states passed a law about not changing the time?

   a. They want to control whether the clocks change in their state.
   b. They are hoping other states will do the same thing.
   c. They don't think a national law is necessary.

6. In this conversation, how do Paul and Fatimah find out when Daylight Saving Time will begin?

a. They look at a calendar app on a phone.
b. They look online at some of the state laws.
c. They ask an expert.

ACTIVITY 2: LEARNING NEW PHRASAL VERBS

Read this information about 3 phrasal verbs. Study the example sentences carefully. To help learn them, read the example sentences aloud or write them on a sheet of paper or in a document.

#61: CUT OFF

61A: remove a part of something

- Every morning my daughter **cuts off** the crust of her toast before she eats it.
- Be careful with that knife or you'll **cut off** your finger!

61B: separate a person, a place, or a thing by isolating them or by stopping something necessary, such as money, air, information, etc.

- I tried to explain what happened, but she **cut** me **off** in the middle of a sentence.
- You can die if your oxygen is **cut off** for more than a few minutes.

#62: PULL UP

62A: retrieve a document or photo on a device (like a phone or computer)

- After several hours, we were able to **pull up** all the files from my computer I thought were lost.
- Let me **pull up** a recent photo of my kids on my phone.

62B: raise to higher position

- These pants are loose, so if I don't wear a belt, I have to keep **pulling** them **up**.
- If you want to **pull up** your grade in biology, you need to study really hard.

62C: drive a car or other vehicle to a certain place and park there

- Can you **pull up** right behind that white car?
- When a police car **pulled up** in front of my neighbor's house, I got really worried.

#63: TURN BACK

63A: go back in the direction you came from; stop from going forward

- I **turned back** as soon as I realized I didn't have my cell phone with me.

- Don't forget your passport so that you are not **turned back** at the border.

63B: go back to the past, especially when talking about *time* or *clocks*

- I had to **turn back** all the clocks in our house this morning because of Daylight Saving Time.
- I wish I could **turn back** time and do that job interview again.

63C: TURN BACK TO: return to something (like a topic) from before

- Class, let's **turn back to** Chapter 7 for a few minutes. On page 142, there is a list of important topics that will be on tomorrow's test.
- Joe, would you **turn back to** the month of January on the calendar? Let's look at those dates again.

ACTIVITY 3: PRACTICING IMPORTANT PHRASES

Give the phrasal verb for the meaning. Be sure to use the correct verb tense.

1. stop a customer's internet = _____ _____ a customer's internet

2. look at Chapter 4 again = _____ _____ _____ Chapter 4
3. raise your socks = _____ _____ your socks
4. drove in front of the restaurant = _____ _____ in front of the restaurant
5. first, you should remove the top of the onion = first, you should _____ _____ the top of the onion

∼

ACTIVITY 4: USING CORRECT PREPOSITIONS

Read the sentences carefully and add the missing prepositions for each phrasal verb.

1. Did you remember to **turn** _____ your clocks last night?
2. As soon as I asked Joe about the money he owes me, he **cut** _____ our conversation.
3. If you want to check your answers, you can **pull** them _____ by going to this link.
4. The plan is to build a dam here that will **cut** _____ the extra water that is flooding the area.
5. When it started to rain, I **turned** _____ and went home.
6. Just as we **pulled** _____ in front of the station, we saw the train leaving.

∼

ACTIVITY 5: VERBS IN CONTEXT

Use the context to select the correct verb for the sentence.

1. If you could (cut off, pull up, turn back, turn back to) time and be any age again, what age would you like to be?
2. When I cook meat, the first thing I do is to (cut off, pull up, turn back, turn back to) any fat I can see.
3. Can you help me (cut off, pull up, turn back) the copy of my research paper that I have in my Google Drive?
4. Sarah had to move out of her nice apartment because her parents (cut off, pulled up, turned back, turned back to) the money they were giving her.
5. The police officer asked everyone to (cut off, pull up, turn back) and go another way to avoid the accident.

ACTIVITY 6: ONLINE PRACTICE

You can practice the phrasal verbs from this lesson at

http://tinyurl.com/33c4nuvr

Here you can use *Flashcards*, *Learn*, or *Match*. You can also have more guided practice with *Q-Chat*, which offers *Teach me*, *Quiz me*, and *Apply my knowledge*.

Answers for Lesson 1

Activity 1

1. c
2. a
3. b
4. c
5. b
6. a

Activity 3

1. cut off
2. turn back to
3. pull up
4. pulled up
5. cut off

Activity 4

1. back
2. off
3. up
4. off
5. back
6. up

Activity 5

1. turn back
2. cut off
3. pull up
4. cut off
5. turned back

LESSON 2
CLEAN UP; SET OUT; SHUT DOWN

ACTIVITY 1: CONVERSATION PRACTICE

A student is talking about his school project.

Read this conversation. Think about the meanings of the **3 new bold verbs**. Remember the meanings of the <u>underlined verbs</u> from earlier lessons. Then answer the comprehension questions.

Mom: Jason, you're going to be late! You aren't ready yet, and the bus will be here in five minutes.
Jason: Okay, okay. I'll make it, Mom. I'm already done eating. I just need to **shut down** my computer, and then I'll go to the bus stop. I wanted to <u>pull up</u> the notes for my presentation for science class one more time and read them again while I was eating breakfast.
Mom: That's a good idea. Remind me, what's the topic?
Jason: Well, we're studying space now. This presentation is about whether people can ever really live on the moon. That's actually not the topic I **set out to** talk about. My first plan was to do a general talk about the moon—you know, things like size, temperature—just general things like that.
Mom: Why did you change the focus?
Jason: I got some good feedback from my teacher. She said my talk was too general and that I needed to talk about something more specific. She suggested I try to answer a question of some kind, so I chose whether people can live on the moon someday.
Mom: And so, what do you think now? Can people live on the moon?
Jason: Well, I know it might sound a little crazy right now, but yeah, I do think it's going to be possible in the future. That's what a lot of the experts say, anyway.

Mom: Interesting. So, do you feel ready to give the presentation this morning?

Jason: Actually, it's not until this afternoon, so I can practice again after lunch. I feel pretty ready. I'm just worried my presentation might be too long, and if I'm more than one minute over the ten-minute time limit, the teacher might <u>cut</u> me <u>off</u>. She did that once before during my presentation about glaciers.

Mom: I'm sure it'll be fine. You'll probably end up talking a little faster once you get up in front of everyone.

Jason: Okay. Just let me **clean up** my breakfast dishes and then I'll be out the door.

Mom: Oh, the bus is <u>pulling up</u> now, so forget about the dishes. Good luck today!

1. What is Jason's mom worried about?

    a. The teacher has given an assignment that Jason can't do.
    b. Jason's presentation is going to be too long.
    c. Jason is going to miss the school bus.

2. What does Jason have to do before he can catch the school bus?

    a. shut down his computer and clean up his dishes
    b. practice his presentation a few more times
    c. cook some eggs for breakfast

3. What question will Jason try to answer in his presentation?

   a. How important are glaciers for life on the moon?
   b. Why will the moon be a great place for children to live?
   c. Will people be able to live on the moon?

4. When will Jason give his presentation?

   a. after lunch
   b. during lunch
   c. before lunch

5. What is Jason worried about?

   a. The teacher has given an assignment that he can't do.
   b. His presentation is going to be too long.
   c. He is going to miss the school bus.

6. What do we know about Jason's teacher?

   a. His teacher believes people will never live on the moon.
   b. His teacher has cut him off during a presentation before.
   c. His teacher always gives him a good grade.

ACTIVITY 2: LEARNING NEW PHRASAL VERBS

Read this information about 3 phrasal verbs. Study the example sentences carefully. To help learn them, read the example sentences aloud or write them on a sheet of paper or in a document.

#64: CLEAN UP

64A: remove dirt or items that do not belong or organize an area to make it look better

- How can we **clean up** the local park?
- Who **cleaned up** the house after the party?

64B: make something nicer so it does not have any dangerous, unacceptable, or controversial parts

- My essay is almost finished, but I want to read it one more time and **clean up** any spelling or punctuation mistakes it might have.
- The writer of that story has decided to **clean up** some of the language in it before she publishes the book.

#65: SET OUT

65A: **SET OUT TO**: make a plan to do something that requires more than just your time or your effort, such as some type of travel or big job

- If **you set out to** do something and then work hard, you will probably meet your goal.
- I didn't **set out to** cook so much pasta, but now I have enough for at least ten people.

65B: **BE SET OUT**: explain details about something in a very clear way, usually in a written document (Note: Usually used in the passive voice.)

- All the assignments for the course **are set out** in the course syllabus.
- The exact price for the car **was set out** in the contract we signed.

#66: SHUT DOWN

66: stop working completely; make something stop working; close something

- Do you **shut down** your computer every time you leave the office?
- When the pilot **shut down** the engines and turned off the seat belt sign, we stood up to get off the plane.

ACTIVITY 3: PRACTICING IMPORTANT PHRASES

Give the phrasal verb for the meaning. Be sure to use the correct verb tense.

1. planned to change voters' opinions = _____ _____ _____ change voters' opinions
2. are explained on page 32 = _____ _____ _____ on page 32
3. when I'm tired, my brain stops working = when I'm tired, my brain _____ _____
4. the ingredients are listed in the recipe = the ingredients _____ _____ _____ in the recipe
5. make the kitchen look better by organizing things = _____ _____ the kitchen

∽

ACTIVITY 4: USING CORRECT PREPOSITIONS

Read the sentences carefully and add the missing prepositions for each phrasal verb.

1. The COVID pandemic **shut** _____ the world.
2. We need a broom and a mop to **clean** _____ this room.
3. I didn't **set** _____ _____ write such a long essay, but now it's over 5,000 words.
4. All the steps you need to take to sell your car without a lawyer are **set** _____ on this website.
5. If you can **clean** _____ the mistakes in this essay, you'll get a better grade.
6. Without additional money, the government will have to **shut** _____ this program.

∽

ACTIVITY 5: VERBS IN CONTEXT

Use the context to select the correct verb for the sentence.

1. Can you please (clean up, are set out, set out to, shut down) this mess?
2. All the details (cleaned up, were set out, set out to, shut down) in the letter you got from the company.
3. I'm glad they finally decided to (clean up, set out, set out to, shut down) the website that caused our computers to crash.
4. The instructions didn't clearly explain how to (clean up, are set out, set out to, shut down) the machines correctly.
5. My plan was to (clean up, are set out, set out to, shut down) my office before I went on vacation, but I didn't have enough time.

ACTIVITY 6: ONLINE PRACTICE

You can practice the phrasal verbs from this lesson at

http://tinyurl.com/9tzv2m8a

Here you can use *Flashcards*, *Learn*, or *Match*. You can also have more guided practice with *Q-Chat*, which offers *Teach me*, *Quiz me*, and *Apply my knowledge*.

Answers for Lesson 2

Activity 1

1. c
2. a
3. c
4. a
5. b
6. b

Activity 3

1. set out to
2. are set out
3. shuts down
4. are set out
5. clean up

Activity 4

1. down
2. up
3. out to
4. out
5. up
6. down

Activity 5

1. clean up
2. were set out
3. shut down
4. shut down
5. clean up

LESSON 3
SLOW DOWN; TURN OVER; WIND UP

ACTIVITY 1: CONVERSATION PRACTICE

Two people are traveling to an event by car.

Read this conversation. Think about the meanings of the **3 new bold verbs**. Remember the meanings of the underlined verbs from earlier lessons. Then answer the comprehension questions.

Sue: Mitch, please **slow down!** I think the street where we're supposed to turn is coming up.
Mitch: Are you sure? I think it's farther ahead. I think it's by the movie theater.
Sue: Let me pull up the directions on my phone again and check.
Mitch: Uh oh.
Sue: What?
Mitch: It looks like there's some kind of problem. I think they've shut down one of the roads. Yes, it looks like the road that's closed is Route 12. That's the road the directions say to follow. Traffic is completely stopped now.
Sue: I just checked the traffic app on my phone, and it says that we should turn back and make a right turn onto State Street. It's about three blocks back. If we do that, we'll **wind up** at an intersection where we can turn onto Route 12 in about five miles.
Mitch: We can see right now what's happening here, so I don't know if I want to **turn over** control of our trip to an app that might not know about Route 12. What do you think?
Sue: Mitch, I hear you, but I think we can trust this app.
Mitch: Okay. Then let's just do what the apps says. I hope it doesn't **slow** us **down** too much. I don't want

to be late for Dave's party. His family worked really hard to arrange everything to surprise him. We need to be on time so we don't ruin the surprise.

Sue: The app says we'll be there in plenty of time. Let's just hope this is the only traffic problem we have.

1. What does Sue ask Mitch to do?

    a. turn on the radio
    b. slow down
    c. find a map

2. What is happening with Route 12?

    a. The road is one way.
    b. The road is not open to cars today.
    c. The road has a lot of traffic today.

3. What does Mitch think of the app?

    a. He is unsure about using it.
    b. He prefers it to a paper map.
    c. He thinks it is wrong.

4. Where are Mitch and Sue going?

    a. to a party
    b. to a movie
    c. We don't know from this conversation.

5. Why are they worried about being late to the party?

   a. They don't want to miss seeing some friends.
   b. They don't want to miss having some cake.
   c. They don't want to ruin the surprise.

6. Do Sue and Mitch think they will make it to the party on time?

   a. They both think they will.
   b. Neither one thinks they will.
   c. Sue does, but Mitch is not sure.

ACTIVITY 2: LEARNING NEW PHRASAL VERBS

Read this information about 3 phrasal verbs. Study the example sentences carefully. To help learn them, read the example sentences aloud or write them on a sheet of paper or in a document.

#67: SLOW DOWN

67: move more slowly than usual or than before

- Every driver should **slow down** when driving past a school.
- A good language teacher will **slow down** when speaking to beginning-level students.

#68: TURN OVER

68A: give control of something to someone else

- When pilots want to take a break, they **turn over** the airplane to the co-pilot.
- When I left my job, I **turned over** my company ID and cell phone to my manager.

68B: flip, like the page of a book or an egg that you are cooking

- I think your burger is burning. You should **turn** it **over** now.
- The driver lost control, and then the car **turned over**.

#69: WIND UP

69: end with a situation that was not planned, especially a situation that is not desirable

- If you studied business, how did you **wind up** teaching high school art?
- We wanted to eat pizza, but we somehow **wound up** at a Chinese restaurant.

ACTIVITY 3: PRACTICING IMPORTANT PHRASES

Give the phrasal verb for the meaning. Be sure to use the correct verb tense.

1. Please don't speak so fast = Please _____ _____
2. flip your ID to look at the back = _____ _____ your ID to look at the back
3. we stayed four days when the plan was to stay two days = we _____ _____ staying four days
4. *Once over* in recipes means you've flipped the egg = *Once over* means you've _____ _____ the egg
5. in the end, we read all five chapters = we _____ _____ reading all five chapters

∼

ACTIVITY 4: USING CORRECT PREPOSITIONS

Read the sentences carefully and add the missing prepositions for each phrasal verb.

1. When you finish playing one side of vinyl, you can **turn** it _____ and play the songs on the other side.
2. Who **wound** _____ meeting your aunt at the airport?
3. When I saw the sign for a school zone, of course I immediately **slowed** _____.
4. Could you please **slow** _____? I can't understand you.
5. He didn't have any money, so I **wound** _____ paying for his dinner, too.

6. The teacher said, "When you've finished your test, will you please **turn** it _____ so I know you're done."

ACTIVITY 5: VERBS IN CONTEXT

Use the context to select the correct verb for the sentence.

1. Hey, you're driving in a school zone. Why don't you (slow down, turn over, wind up) a bit, okay?
2. When I (slowed down, turned over, wound up) my paper and saw the grade, I was really happy.
3. When the taxi began to (slow down, turn over, wind up), I knew we were close to our hotel.
4. If you don't want to (slow down, turn over, wind up) working as a street cleaner your whole life, you need to graduate from high school.
5. When I (slowed down, turned over, wound up) the back cover of the book, I saw a photo of the author.

ACTIVITY 6: ONLINE PRACTICE

You can practice the phrasal verbs from this lesson at

http://tinyurl.com/3xpcsc4a

Here you can use *Flashcards*, *Learn*, or *Match*. You can also have more guided practice with *Q-Chat*, which offers *Teach me*, *Quiz me*, and *Apply my knowledge*.

Answers for Lesson 3

Activity 1

1. b
2. b
3. a
4. a
5. c
6. a

Activity 3

1. slow down
2. turn over
3. wound up
4. turned over
5. wound up

Activity 4

1. over
2. up
3. down
4. down
5. up
6. over

Activity 5

1. slow down
2. turned over
3. slow down
4. wind up
5. turned over

LESSON 4
LAY OUT; TAKE BACK; TURN UP

ACTIVITY 1: CONVERSATION PRACTICE

Some people are discussing some plans to expand the library.

Read this conversation. Think about the meanings of the **3 new bold verbs**. Remember the meanings of the <u>underlined verbs</u> from earlier lessons. Then answer the comprehension questions.

Sandy: Thank you for meeting with me today, Joe. We're excited to see the plans for the library expansion.
Joe: Sure, let me **lay out** the latest set of designs, and let's see what you think.
Sandy: Oh, wow. They look great! People will be so happy to have more space for all the events we want to have in the future. This place offers so many benefits for the city, but we outgrew this space years ago.
Joe: As you can see, we've increased the size of the space for events, so you can include more people when authors come to speak about their books. And with the extra room we added, you'll <u>wind up</u> having enough room even if another 50 or 60 people **turn up**.
Sandy: That looks great! Hey, I wonder if you could add some counter space and also space for a refrigerator for the caterers. They love having a room where they can <u>set out</u> everything and prepare the food. That kind of space also helps the <u>cleaning up</u> go much faster.
Joe: Well, right now, it isn't designed for that, but I could **take** the plans **back** to my office and make those changes pretty easily. It will add to the cost, of course.
Sandy: I understand.
Joe: I'll let you know the new cost.
Sandy: Great. What about the timing? Will this change <u>slow</u> things <u>down</u> very much? We need to stay on

schedule so that the city book festival can use this space next year.

Joe: Not at all. It should only take a day for me to get the revised designs to you. Is there anything else you want me to change?

Sandy: No, that's it. I'll show the plans to our library board with the revised costs so we can get things started as soon as possible.

Joe: Sounds good.

1. What is going to happen to the library?

    a. It is going to be sold.
    b. It is going to be made bigger.
    c. It is going to have a new roof.

2. What do the caterers need?

    a. a space to read
    b. a space for sitting
    c. a space to prepare food for events

3. Why isn't the design final?

    a. Sandy doesn't like the design.
    b. Some items need to be added to one room.
    c. The current design costs too much money.

4. When will the revised designs be ready?

   a. in a month
   b. in a few days
   c. We don't know from this conversation.

5. What is happening next year?

   a. The city's book festival will use the new space.
   b. The designer will have the new plans ready.
   c. The library will close permanently.

6. What is Sandy worried about?

   a. The library will become too crowded.
   b. The book festival will not be popular.
   c. The changes to the library will take too long.

ACTIVITY 2: LEARNING NEW PHRASAL VERBS

Read this information about 3 phrasal verbs. Study the example sentences carefully. To help learn them, read the example sentences aloud or write them on a sheet of paper or in a document.

#70: LAY OUT

70A: explain the details very clearly (Note: Similar in meaning to **65B. SET OUT**)

- The contract **lays out** the sales price of your house.
- The new plan **laid out** the steps the company would take to make more money next year.

70B: arrange or display in a certain way (according to a plan, usually)

- When I try to put together a puzzle, the first thing I always do is to **lay out** all the pieces on the table and look for similar colors.
- When I entered the room, the cards were already **laid out** on the table.

#71: TAKE BACK

71A: get possession of something you had before

- Jenny finished using my laptop, so I'm **taking** it **back** now.
- I lent James my tennis racket, but I **took** it **back** so I could play tomorrow.

71B: return something to its original place

- This shirt is too big, so I think I'm going to **take** it **back** to the store for a smaller size.
- Before we check in for the flight, we'll have to **take back** the rental car to the rental office.

#72: TURN UP

72A: increase the volume or intensity of a radio, TV, stove, or other machine

- Can you **turn up** the TV?
- If you **turn up** the heat, the food will cook faster.

72B: be in a place, often surprisingly or unexpectedly

- How many people **turned up** for the meeting?
- My sister **turned up** at the airport when we arrived last night.

ACTIVITY 3: PRACTICING IMPORTANT PHRASES

Give the phrasal verb for the meaning. Be sure to use the correct verb tense.

1. increase the sound of the music = _____ _____ the music
2. explain the reasons for doing something = _____ _____ the reasons for doing something
3. get your car again = _____ _____ your car
4. 10 people attended the meeting = 10 people _____ _____ at the meeting
5. arrange the presentation slides = _____ _____ the presentation slides

ACTIVITY 4: USING CORRECT PREPOSITIONS

Read the sentences carefully and add the missing prepositions for each phrasal verb.

1. Before I start a jigsaw puzzle, I like to **lay** _____ all the pieces on the table first.
2. My ride-share driver never **turned** _____, so I had to take the bus.
3. She **turned** _____ the heat on the oven so the meat would cook faster.
4. He **took** the dog _____ to the shelter because it was biting everyone.
5. Our coach **laid** _____ the game plan for each of us.
6. Over 50 people **turned** _____ at her 80th birthday party!

ACTIVITY 5: VERBS IN CONTEXT

Use the context to select the correct verb for the sentence.

1. If you don't like this computer, you can (lay it out, take it back, turn it up) to the store.
2. All the items I needed for the recipe were (laid out, taken back, turned up) on the counter for me.
3. I love this song! Will you (lay out, take back, turn up) the volume?

4. Did you already (lay out, take back, turn up) the library book?
5. (Laying out, Taking back, Turning up) early for your first day of work is a good thing to do.

ACTIVITY 6: ONLINE PRACTICE

You can practice the phrasal verbs from this lesson at

http://tinyurl.com/2dszvyxw

Here you can use *Flashcards*, *Learn*, or *Match*. You can also have more guided practice with *Q-Chat*, which offers *Teach me*, *Quiz me*, and *Apply my knowledge*.

Answers for Lesson 4

Activity 1

1. b
2. c
3. b
4. b
5. a
6. c

Activity 3

1. turn up
2. lay out
3. take back
4. turned up
5. lay out

Activity 4

1. out
2. 2. up
3. 3. up
4. 4. back
5. 5. out
6. 6. up

Activity 5

1. 1. take it back
2. 2. laid out
3. 3. turn up
4. 4. take back
5. 5. Turning up

LESSON 5
GO OVER; HOLD ON; LINE UP

ACTIVITY 1: CONVERSATION PRACTICE

A class is taking a trip to the museum.

Read this conversation. Think about the meanings of the **3 new bold verbs**. Remember the meanings of the <u>underlined</u>

verbs from earlier lessons. Then answer the comprehension questions.

Rita (teacher): Good morning, everyone. I'm glad so many of you are here today for our field trip to the natural history museum. I'm sure you're really excited to learn more about dinosaurs!

Kathy (aide to teacher): Okay, class, we're ready to go in. Please **line up** to get your tickets so we can start the tour.

Rita: Everyone, I just want to remind you that there are a few rules while we're in the museum. I'm going to **go over** them now. First, remember not to talk while the tour guide is talking. If you have a question, raise your hand, just like in class. Then you can ask your question. Next, please stay with the group. We don't want anyone to wind up getting lost. At the end of the tour, we'll have a snack in the museum cafeteria. And before we leave, we'll visit the museum's gift shop.

Will (student): How long will the tour last?

Rita: About 30 minutes. I'm going to turn over the class to the tour guide, whose name is Tracy. Be sure to pay attention because there will be a quiz on some of this information tomorrow. Okay, I think we're ready to start the tour.

Kathy: **Hold on,** everyone. Sorry to cut you off, Rita, but I just found a hat. Did anyone lose a hat?

Lily (student): I think that's mine. Oh, I'm glad it turned up! My mom got it. She would have been really mad if I lost it.

Kathy: Well, I'm glad we found it, Lily.

Will: What did the dinosaurs eat?
Kathy: Will, that's a really good question, but right now it's time to listen. The tour guide will answer that question during the tour.
Rita: Okay, let's find out about dinosaurs now!

1. When does this conversation take place?

    a. after the tour
    b. during the tour
    c. before the tour

2. What is the main activity of the field trip?

    a. having a snack
    b. visiting a gift shop
    c. seeing dinosaurs

3. What should students NOT do during the tour?

    a. ask questions
    b. leave the group
    c. take photos

4. In what order will things happen at the museum?

    a. They will visit the gift shop, tour the museum, and then eat snacks.
    b. They will tour the museum, eat snacks, and then visit the gift shop.

c. They will eat snacks, tour the museum, and then visit the gift shop.

5. What is Tracy's job?

   a. She is a teacher.
   b. She is an aide to the teacher.
   c. She is a tour guide.

6. Who lost a hat?

   a. Lily
   b. Will
   c. two students

∼

ACTIVITY 2: LEARNING NEW PHRASAL VERBS

Read this information about 3 phrasal verbs. Study the example sentences carefully. To help learn them, read the example sentences aloud or write them on a sheet of paper or in a document.

#73: GO OVER

73A: GO OVER TO: move in the direction of a place or a person by crossing an area such as in a room

- The teacher asked the students to **go over to** the window.

- She **went over to** her neighbor's house to have coffee and to talk.

73B: examine something in great detail to remember it or to make sure it is correct

- The police are **going over** everything that the witnesses said.
- Before the test, I **went over** my notes carefully.

#74: HOLD ON

74A: wait for a short period of time; usually a spoken request

- Could you **hold on** a minute? I need to make a quick call.
- **Hold on**! I need to grab my jacket before we go out.

74B: **HOLD ON TO**: refuse to let go of something

- **Hold on to** the railing or you might fall!
- **Hold on to** your dreams and never give up on them!

#75: LINE UP

75A: form a line

- There are at least 50 people **lined up** in front of the store now.
- The passengers **lined up** to enter the plane.

75B: put or organize things in a row or line

- My mother **lines up** all of her vitamins and medications so she doesn't forget any.
- All of my shoes are **lined up** by the door.

75C: arrange something successfully

- My niece in high school has already **lined up** a great summer job.
- Jackie and Thomas **lined up** a babysitter for Friday night.

ACTIVITY 3: PRACTICING IMPORTANT PHRASES

Give the phrasal verb for the meaning. Be sure to use the correct verb tense.

1. keeping a hand on the rope = ____ ____ ____ the rope
2. put things in a row by size = ____ ____ things by size
3. review the instructions again = ____ ____ the instructions again
4. setting up plans for a trip = ____ ____ plans for a trip
5. moving to a specific place = ____ ____ ____ a specific place

ACTIVITY 4: USING CORRECT PREPOSITIONS

Read the sentences carefully and add the missing prepositions for each phrasal verb.

1. Please **hold** _____ while I check flight's status on the computer.
2. Are people **lining** _____ already to get into the theater?
3. Let's **go** _____ your test results again.
4. **Holding** _____ _____ the railing when it's icy out is good advice.
5. Are you ready to **go** _____ _____ the park to see the fireworks?
6. I just **lined** _____ a beautiful place for the wedding next year.

ACTIVITY 5: VERBS IN CONTEXT

Use the context to select the correct verb for the sentence.

1. Please (go over to, hold on, line up) the bookshelf and get the big dictionary.
2. Before our trip next week, we really need to (go over, hold on, line up) at least three restaurants for group dinners.

3. They (went over to, held on, lined up) the other side of the stadium to get a better seat for the tennis match.
4. The teacher asked the students to (go over, hold on, line up) alphabetically.
5. Please (go over, hold on, line up) just a minute while I zip up my coat.

ACTIVITY 6: ONLINE PRACTICE

You can practice the phrasal verbs from this lesson at

http://tinyurl.com/y83fnyzw

Here you can use *Flashcards*, *Learn*, or *Match*. You can also have more guided practice with *Q-Chat*, which offers *Teach me*, *Quiz me*, and *Apply my knowledge*.

Answers for Lesson 5

Activity 1

1. c
2. b
3. b
4. b
5. c
6. a

Activity 3

1. holding on to
2. line up
3. go over
4. lining up
5. going over to

Activity 4

1. on
2. up
3. over to
4. on to
5. over
6. up

Activity 5

1. go over
2. line up
3. went over
4. line up
5. hold on

LESSON 6
GO THROUGH; HANG UP; PAY OFF

ACTIVITY 1: CONVERSATION PRACTICE

A man talks to his friend about getting a new job.

Read this conversation. Think about the meanings of the **3 new bold verbs**. Remember the meanings of the underlined verbs from earlier lessons. Then answer the comprehension questions.

Matt: Hey, Andy, how are you?
Andy: Well, honestly, I'm kind of in a bad mood today.
Matt: What's up?
Andy: I guess I'm still mad about what happened to me at work last month. I can't stop thinking about it.
Matt: Really, are you still **hung up** on that? Andy, I know what happened wasn't right, but I think it's time for you to either forget it or decide to find another place to work.
Andy: I know you're right. But I put in so many long hours and weekends over so many years! I can't believe that all that hard work didn't **pay off** for me there.
Matt: I know how hard you worked there, but you also **went through** a lot because of your boss. It's just not right. You deserve so much better.
Andy: I agree. Okay, so what do you think I should do first if I want to change jobs?
Matt: Well, I think it's time to line up some interviews, even if they are just about getting information about other companies. Start with companies in your field, maybe even some of your company's competitors. Those companies will recognize how experienced you are.
Andy: I guess that makes sense. I know a few people I can talk to. I'll try to do that right away.

Matt: Hey, one of my college friends is a headhunter. Let me text her and see if she can help you.
Andy: That's nice of you. I've never worked with a headhunter before. Do I have to pay her?
Matt: Usually the companies that are hiring pay the headhunter. Even if the headhunter can't help you, she can probably give you some tips for your resume and preparing for interviews.
Andy: Sounds good.
Matt: And I'd be happy to go over your resume, too. I see a lot of resumes in my job. After you update it, we can check to make sure that everything is laid out okay. You need to be sure it will look good if someone sees it on their phone because that's how resumes are often viewed now—not just on computers. Things have changed a lot since you got your current job.
Andy: It sounds like it. Thanks, Matt, I'm really grateful for all the advice. Thank you so much for helping me move on.

1. What happened to Andy at work?

    a. He lost his job and is no longer working there.
    b. His boss gave him a bad job evaluation.
    c. He experienced something he thought was unfair.

2. What is Andy going to do next?

    a. He is going to call a headhunter.
    b. He is going to make appointments for interviews.
    c. He is going to start a new job.

3. Which of these statements is false?

   a. Matt tells Andy to start looking for a new job.
   b. Matt tells Andy to find a way to stay in his current job.
   c. Matt tells Andy to interview headhunters to help him.

4. How will Matt help Andy?

   a. He will review his resume.
   b. He will pay for the headhunter.
   c. He will find him a new profession.

5. How will people read Andy's updated resume?

   a. on computers and phones
   b. only on phones
   c. only on computers

6. What is Matt's job?

   a. He is a headhunter.
   b. He writes resumes.
   c. We don't know from this conversation.

ACTIVITY 2: LEARNING NEW PHRASAL VERBS

Read this information about 3 phrasal verbs. Study the example sentences carefully. To help learn them, read the example sentences aloud or write them on a sheet of paper or in a document.

#76: GO THROUGH

76A: experience a process, often one that includes something difficult or sometimes unpleasant feelings

- John is **going through** a difficult time and really needs his friends now.
- The players are **going through** a training program that starts at 6 a.m. every day.

76B: study or inspect a thing or a place very carefully

- Our lawyer is **going through** the new contract now.
- We **went through** all of the boxes and files in the basement after my dad died.

76C: GO THROUGH WITH: start and finish an action that you thought was difficult or unpleasant

- Sarah always talked about quitting her job, and yesterday she finally **went through with** it.
- If the phone company **goes through with** their new plan, my phone bill will increase by 20%.

#77: HANG UP

77A: end a phone call

- The connection was bad, so I decided to **hang up** and call again.
- Jonathan **hung up** while I was trying to explain what happened.

77B: put something on a hook or a hanger

- You can **hang up** your coat in the bedroom closet.
- My uncle **hung up** his towel on the hook in the bathroom.

77C: **BE HUNG UP ON:** be bothered by something or someone and spend a lot of time thinking about it or them

- A lot of people **are hung up on** what other people think about them.
- Michael won't buy that car because he **is hung up on** the price.

#78: PAY OFF

78A: pay the complete amount of money that you owe for something

- It is important to **pay off** your credit card bill each month.

- Most people take 20 years or longer to **pay off** their home loans.

78B: have good results from working hard

- If you study English every day, your work will **pay off**.
- All that training finally **paid off** when Maria won the tournament.

ACTIVITY 3: PRACTICING IMPORTANT PHRASES

Give the phrasal verb for the meaning. Be sure to use the correct verb tense.

1. look in the boxes = _____ _____ the boxes
2. is unable to get past something = _____ _____ _____ _____ something
3. put your coat in the closet = _____ _____ your coat in the closet
4. finish paying a loan = _____ _____ a loan
5. endure a difficult time = _____ _____ a difficult time

ACTIVITY 4: USING CORRECT PREPOSITIONS

Read the sentences carefully and add the missing prepositions for each phrasal verb.

1. Did you **go** _____ _____ the plan to sell your business?
2. **Paying** _____ my school loans is my top priority once I get a job.
3. Don't get **hung** _____ _____ that one bad test score. You'll do better the next time.
4. Don't **hang** _____ yet! I have one more funny story from my trip to tell you.
5. Let's **go** _____ the loan paperwork one more time to make sure it's right.
6. Congratulations! All that practice has **paid** _____. You won the tournament!

~

ACTIVITY 5: VERBS IN CONTEXT

Use the context to select the correct verb for the sentence.

1. Why can't you (go through, go through with, hang up, pay off) your clothes before you go to bed?
2. Have you talked to Sara today? She's (going through, going through with, hung up with, paying off) such a tough time.

3. All that running is finally (going through, going through with, hanging up, paying off). I've lost 15 pounds.
4. Will you (go through, go through with, hang up, pay off) the boxes in the garage and see what we should sell?
5. I've got to (go through, go through with, hang up, pay off) now because my dinner is ready.

ACTIVITY 6: ONLINE PRACTICE

You can practice the phrasal verbs from this lesson at

http://tinyurl.com/ybhxppx3

Here you can use *Flashcards*, *Learn*, or *Match*. You can also have more guided practice with *Q-Chat*, which offers *Teach me*, *Quiz me*, and *Apply my knowledge*.

Answers for Lesson 6

Activity 1

1. c
2. b
3. a
4. a
5. a
6. c

Activity 3

1. go through
2. is hung up on
3. hang up
4. pay off
5. go through

Activity 4

1. through with
2. off
3. up on
4. up
5. through
6. off

Activity 5

1. hang up
2. going through
3. paying off
4. go through
5. hang up

LESSON 7
BREAK UP; HOLD OUT; PULL BACK

ACTIVITY 1: CONVERSATION PRACTICE

Two women are talking about their friend.

Read this conversation. Think about the meanings of the **3 new bold verbs**. Remember the meanings of the underlined verbs from earlier lessons. Then answer the comprehension questions.

Amy: Did you hear what happened yesterday?
Jackie: No. What happened?
Amy: Diana **broke up** with Lucas.
Jackie: What? Why?
Amy: I'm not sure why exactly, but I can tell you how it happened.
Jackie: Tell me.
Amy: Well, Lucas turned up at our house late last night. I saw him standing there on the porch, **holding out** a bouquet of roses to Diana. And when he started talking, she cut him off and told him that she thought they needed to **break up.** And just like that, it was over. He turned around and left.
Jackie: Oh my gosh! I wonder what made her do that. They dated for a long time! How's she doing now?
Amy: She didn't want to talk about it last night, but this morning she told me that she felt she needed to **pull back** from Lucas and their relationship. He wanted her to spend more time with him.
Jackie: Well, she's going through a lot right now, with her brother's illness, her new job, and paying off her college loans. I think she needs to focus on her own life right now. It's too bad that Lucas didn't understand that.
Amy: Yes. I think she'll be happier without him, but right now she might need to be with some friends.

Why don't we see if we can convince her to come out dancing with us on Saturday night?

Jackie: Good idea. Let's invite her. We all need to have some fun.

1. What happened yesterday?

    a. One person broke her arm.
    b. Two coworkers had a fight.
    c. A couple broke up.

2. Where did Diana see Lucas?

    a. in front of the house
    b. in the office
    c. on the bus

3. What did Lucas bring to Diana?

    a. some flowers
    b. some candy
    c. a ring

4. Who is sick now?

    a. Diana
    b. Diana's brother
    c. Lucas

5. What do we learn about Diana at the end of the conversation?

a. She has been sick.
   b. She has student loans.
   c. She doesn't have a job.

6. What will Amy and Jackie do this weekend?

   a. They will go dancing.
   b. They will go to the park.
   c. They will go to the hospital.

∽

ACTIVITY 2: LEARNING NEW PHRASAL VERBS

Read this information about 3 phrasal verbs. Study the example sentences carefully. To help learn them, read the example sentences aloud or write them on a sheet of paper or in a document.

#79: BREAK UP

79A: BREAK UP (WITH): end something like a relationship

- Matt and I decided to **break up** after being together five years.
- After she **broke up with** Jon, Sarah moved to California.

79B: BREAK UP (INTO): divide into smaller or manageable pieces

- Writing an essay is easier if you **break** it **up into** smaller steps.
- I **broke up** the chocolate bar so I could share it with everyone.

79C: separate the people in a crowd or stop the people in a fight

- My uncle is always **breaking up** fights between his two sons.
- The police quickly **broke up** the crowd after the protest.

#80: HOLD OUT

80A: extend; display

- If you **hold out** your hand, I will give you a cookie.
- I **held out** my cell phone so the woman could check my ticket.

80B: HOLD OUT (FOR): wait or delay for something better

- Are you **holding out for** a higher salary?
- The strike is already two weeks old. If the workers **hold out** too long, they may lose their jobs.

#81: PULL BACK

81: move something or oneself backward or away from a place or a person

- When I **pulled back** the curtain, I saw the window was cracked.
- The girl started to run into the street, but her mom **pulled** her **back**.

ACTIVITY 3: PRACTICING IMPORTANT PHRASES

Give the phrasal verb for the meaning. Be sure to use the correct verb tense.

1. waiting for a promotion = ____ ____ ____ a promotion
2. stop an argument = ____ ____ an argument
3. the car moved away from the curb = the car ____ ____ from the curb
4. put your hand out in front of you to show the ring = ____ your hand ____ to show the ring
5. Jo and Dan stopped dating each other = Jo and Dan ____ ____

ACTIVITY 4: USING CORRECT PREPOSITIONS

Read the sentences carefully and add the missing prepositions for each phrasal verb.

1. It's hard to **break** _____ _____ someone you've been dating for a long time.
2. We **held** _____ hope that the storm would pass quickly.
3. I was glad to see that the principal **broke** _____ the fight between the students so quickly.
4. When I **pulled** _____ the curtains, I saw how much snow was on the ground.
5. After my shoulder injury, I wasn't able to **hold** my arms _____ straight.
6. The captain **pulled** all of the soldiers _____ from the front line.

∼

ACTIVITY 5: VERBS IN CONTEXT

Use the context to select the correct verb for the sentence.

1. Sorry, but I accidentally broke the knife when I was (breaking up, hold up, pulling back) the block of ice.
2. The union announced they were (breaking up, holding out, pulling back) for better health benefits.
3. When I (broke up, held out, pulled back) my hand, everyone could clearly see my finger was broken.
4. They were still (breaking up, holding out, pulling back) hope that the new treatment would work and save his life.
5. After a few miles, one of the cyclists (broke up, held out, pulled back) from the riders in the front.

ACTIVITY 6: ONLINE PRACTICE

You can practice the phrasal verbs from this lesson at

http://tinyurl.com/4dz4pyxu

Here you can use *Flashcards*, *Learn*, or *Match*. You can also have more guided practice with *Q-Chat*, which offers *Teach me*, *Quiz me*, and *Apply my knowledge*.

Answers for Lesson 7

Activity 1

1. c
2. a
3. c
4. b
5. b
6. a

Activity 3

1. holding out for
2. break up
3. pulled back
4. hold out
5. broke up

Activity 4

1. up with
2. out
3. up
4. back
5. out
6. back

Activity 5

1. breaking up
2. holding out
3. held out
4. holding out
5. pulled back

LESSON 8
BRING OUT; BUILD UP; HANG ON

ACTIVITY 1: CONVERSATION PRACTICE

Two people are trying a new restaurant.

Read this conversation. Think about the meanings of the **3 new bold verbs**. Remember the meanings of the <u>underlined verbs</u> from earlier lessons. Then answer the comprehension questions.

> **Max**: I'm so glad we're getting a chance to eat in this new Greek restaurant! I've been meaning to try it since it first opened.
> **Erica**: Thank you for inviting me! I went to Greece last year, and I really enjoyed the food there. Everything was so fresh and delicious.
> **Max**: t sounds wonderful! I'd like to go there someday.
> **Erica**: The restaurants here are not, of course, as good as in Greece, but whenever I eat Greek food, it brings back a lot of great memories. I had so many amazing meals when I was there, especially on Crete.
> **Max**: How long were you there?
> **Erica**: Two weeks. I don't think I had a bad meal the entire time.
> **Max**: Well, I hope this meal will be just as good. This is my first time in this part of town. It's getting so **built up** with apartments and, of course, a lot of great restaurants.
> **Erica**: Yes, it is. Hey, I'm ready to order. Are you?
> **Max**: Yes. What are you having?
> **Erica**: I'm getting the spinach pie and the grilled octopus.
> **Max**: That sounds good. I think I'll get that, too!
> [30 minutes later]
> **Max**: Gosh, it's taking a really long time to get our food. Maybe coming here was a mistake.

Erica: It's also really cold in here. I'm glad I **hung on** to my coat, but I wish I had ordered the Greek lemon chicken soup. It would warm me up.
Max: Yeah, soup would be nice right now. What's that soup called again?
Erica: Avgolemono. It's so good! Hey, it looks like the waiter is **bringing out** our food right now.
Max: Finally!

Max: This food is SO good! I am going to take back what I said about the long wait. It was worth it!
Erica: This is the best Greek food I've had since I got back from my trip.
Max: We are definitely going to be coming back here to eat again!

1. Why are Max and Erica eating at this restaurant?

   a. They love Greek food.
   b. Their families are Greek.
   c. They live in this area of the city.

2. What does Max want?

   a. to get his coat
   b. to go to Greece sometime
   c. to leave the restaurant

3. Who ordered the octopus?

   a. Erica
   b. Max
   c. Erica and Max

4. What does Erica wish?

   a. that she had kept her coat
   b. that she was still in Crete
   c. that she had ordered the Greek soup

5. What happened at the restaurant?

   a. Max and Erica got their food quickly.
   b. Max and Erica enjoyed the food.
   c. Max and Erica left early because it was cold.

6. Will Max and Erica come back to this restaurant?

   a. definitely
   b. probably not
   c. We don't know from this conversation.

ACTIVITY 2: LEARNING NEW PHRASAL VERBS

Read this information about 3 phrasal verbs. Study the example sentences carefully. To help learn them, read the example sentences aloud or write them on a sheet of paper or in a document.

#82: BRING OUT

82A: put something in front of or show to others

- Whenever our dog finds something new, she immediately **brings** it **out** and puts it on the floor by the front door.
- My little nephew **brought out** his new toy to show us.

82B: emphasize a detail, quality, or feeling so that it becomes much more noticeable

- The dark green frame **brings out** the colors in that painting.
- I think the arrival of spring **brings out** the best in people.

#83: BUILD UP

83: increase in size or power

- The doctor says you need to **build up** your strength before returning to work.
- Ice began to **build up** on the wing of the plane.

#84: HANG ON

84A: wait for a short period of time

- **Hang on!** Let me get my coat and I'll go with you.
- If you can **hang on** a bit, I'll see if my boss can meet with you soon, okay?

84B: **HANG ON (TO)**: hold tightly; decide to keep

- Okay, the boat is going through some rough water now. **Hang on!**
- I was going to sell this book, but I think I'm going to **hang on to** it instead.

84C: not give up; continue to try (to reach a certain goal)

- **Hang on** a bit longer. I know things are hard now, but when you graduate from college, you'll get a better job and things will be different.
- He **hung on to** the hope that he would be offered his dream job.

ACTIVITY 3: PRACTICING IMPORTANT PHRASES

Give the phrasal verb for the meaning. Be sure to use the correct verb tense.

1. made the colors brighter = _____ _____ the colors
2. increase your strength = _____ _____ your strength
3. Can you wait for just a minute? = Can you _____ _____ for just a minute?
4. the police showed their evidence = the police _____ _____ their evidence
5. over time, muscle can increase = over time, muscle can _____ _____

∽

ACTIVITY 4: USING CORRECT PREPOSITIONS

Read the sentences carefully and add the missing prepositions for each phrasal verb.

1. By walking every day, I was able to **build** _____ my stamina and my health.
2. Can you **hang** _____ while I put my boots on?
3. Every year, I can't wait to **bring** my Christmas decorations _____ of storage.
4. Those new glasses look good! They really **bring** _____ your blue eyes.
5. Our new marketing campaign is designed to **build** _____ our customer base.
6. Be sure to **hang** _____ _____ your receipt in case you want to return that shirt.

∽

ACTIVITY 5: VERBS IN CONTEXT

Use the context to select the correct verb for the sentence.

1. Look at the beautiful salad the chef is (bringing out, building up, hanging on) to us now.
2. The new vaccine will help (bring out, build up, hang on) your immunity.
3. I didn't think I could (bring out, build up, hang on, hang on to) without heat much longer, and then the power suddenly came back on.
4. During the cold weather last week, the ice (brought out, built up, hung on) on the trees pretty fast.
5. Unfortunately, we found our kitten (bringing out, building up, hanging on, hanging on to) the curtain with his claws.

ACTIVITY 6: ONLINE PRACTICE

You can practice the phrasal verbs from this lesson at

http://tinyurl.com/5du58e6e

Here you can use *Flashcards*, *Learn*, or *Match*. You can also have more guided practice with *Q-Chat*, which offers *Teach me*, *Quiz me*, and *Apply my knowledge*.

Answers for Lesson 8

Activity 1

1. a
2. b
3. c
4. c
5. b
6. a

Activity 3

1. brought out
2. build up
3. hang on
4. brought out
5. build up

Activity 4

1. up
2. on
3. out
4. out
5. up
6. on to

Activity 5

1. bringing out
2. build up
3. hang on
4. built up
5. hanging on to

LESSON 9
GET DOWN; PUT ON; THROW OUT

ACTIVITY 1: CONVERSATION PRACTICE

A man is telling his neighbor about some changes he is making to his house.

Read this conversation. Think about the meanings of the **3 new bold verbs**. Remember the meanings of the <u>underlined verbs</u> from earlier lessons. Then answer the comprehension questions.

Mike: Hey, Tom, can you help me with this?
Tom: Yes, <u>hang on</u> just a second. I'll help. It looks heavy. What are you doing?
Mike: I'm **throwing out** a lot of things before the workers get started on my house tomorrow. Thanks for the help.
Tom: No problem. What kind of work are they going to do?
Mike: First, they're putting down new carpeting in all the bedrooms and the hallway upstairs. That work starts early tomorrow morning.
Tom: Oh, that's going to look so nice. Do you have to <u>clean up</u> any more parts of the house or are you done now?
Mike: I think I'm done. I'm excited to see and feel the new carpeting. You know how soft the new carpeting can be.
Tom: Yes, I do. It's like walking on a cloud! Are they doing any other work?
Mike: They're going to **put on** a fresh coat of paint later in the week. Then the walls will look as nice as the new carpets. We decided to change paint colors in almost all of the rooms. In my daughter's room, though, we're keeping the walls the same color.
Tom: I'm sure those bedrooms are going to look great once everything is done.

Mike: Yes, I just bought some new artwork for those rooms, too. I put it all in the attic, and so I'll need to **get** it all **down** at some point.
Tom: Well, let me know if you need any help with that. I'm around this weekend and just next door.
Mike: Thanks. I will.

1. What is Mike throwing out?

    a. old artwork
    b. old carpeting
    c. We don't know from this conversation.

2. What is happening tomorrow?

    a. The bedrooms are being painted.
    b. New carpet is being installed.
    c. New artwork is being put on the walls.

3. What is Mike excited about?

    a. how many things he can throw out
    b. how the new paint will smell
    c. how the new carpeting will feel

4. What is the order of the work being done at Mike's house?

    a. painting and then carpeting
    b. carpeting and then painting
    c. hanging new paintings and then carpeting

5. What color are they painting most of the rooms?

   a. light gray
   b. gray
   c. We don't know from this conversation.

6. How do Mike and Tom know each other?

   a. They are neighbors.
   b. They are friends from work.
   c. We don't know from this conversation.

ACTIVITY 2: LEARNING NEW PHRASAL VERBS

Read this information about 3 phrasal verbs. Study the example sentences carefully. To help learn them, read the example sentences aloud or write them on a sheet of paper or in a document.

#85: GET DOWN

85A: move or go lower

- It wasn't hard for the cat to **get down** from the tree when he got hungry.
- Can you **get down** my suitcase from that shelf?

85B: GET DOWN TO: start to pay very careful attention to something

- Yes, Andy likes to have a good time, but when it's time to **get down to** business, he is very motivated and incredibly hard-working.
- Susan was laughing until we **got down to** the details of the contract, and then she was serious and focused.

#86: PUT ON

86A: begin to wear or attach to something

- As soon as I get into a car, I **put on** my seatbelt.
- I saw a woman **putting on** her makeup while she was driving!

86B: present something to watch or listen to

- My son's kindergarten class **put on** a play about animals in a zoo.
- Let's **put on** some music we can dance to!

86C: gain weight (or similar)

- In the winter, I don't exercise as much, so of course I **put on** a few pounds.
- I saw Jonah yesterday for the first time in two years. I was surprised to see how much weight he's **put on**.

#87: THROW OUT

87A: put in the garbage or trash; reject or eliminate

- Can you **throw out** those old newspapers?
- I don't think we should **throw out** everything from the last plan because the first part is really good.

87B: mention or suggest something as a possible thing to do

- Let me **throw out** this idea for our honeymoon: Portugal and the Azores.
- She **threw out** a few suggestions for the name of the new company.

87C: make someone leave a place

- They **threw** my cousin **out** of the movie because he was talking too loudly.
- If you don't sit down, the teacher's going to **throw** you **out** of class.

ACTIVITY 3: PRACTICING IMPORTANT PHRASES

Give the phrasal verb for the meaning. Be sure to use the correct verb tense.

1. wore the new shoes = _____ _____ the new shoes
2. disposed of the old batteries = _____ _____ the old batteries
3. move the box from that shelf = _____ the box _____ from that shelf
4. provide new ideas = _____ _____ new ideas
5. presented the play *Our Town* = _____ _____ the play *Our Town*

∿

ACTIVITY 4: USING CORRECT PREPOSITIONS

Read the sentences carefully and add the missing prepositions for each phrasal verb.

1. Were you able to **get** _____ to basement before the tornado hit?
2. There was so much snow we had to **put** _____ our boots.
3. Don't **throw** _____ that banana! I can use it in my smoothie tomorrow.
4. Sam **put** _____ some romantic music when his date arrived.
5. Once the lawyer got to the meeting, we immediately **got** _____ _____ business.
6. It's common to **put** _____ some weight when you go away to university.

∿

ACTIVITY 5: VERBS IN CONTEXT

Use the context to select the correct verb for the sentence.

1. At the meeting, I (got down, put on, threw out) a few ideas, but no one liked them.
2. Did the temperature (get down, put on, throw out) below freezing here last night?
3. I wasn't happy after my boss (got down, put on, threw out) my proposal for the new design.
4. (Getting down, Putting on, Throwing out) the Christmas play is fun.
5. No matter what I try, my kitten refuses to (get down, put on, throw out) from the kitchen counter.

ACTIVITY 6: ONLINE PRACTICE

You can practice the phrasal verbs from this lesson at

http://tinyurl.com/yuvuxc63

Here you can use *Flashcards*, *Learn*, or *Match*. You can also have more guided practice with *Q-Chat*, which offers *Teach me*, *Quiz me*, and *Apply my knowledge*.

Answers for Lesson 9

Activity 1

1. c
2. b
3. c
4. b
5. c
6. a

Activity 3

1. put on
2. threw out
3. get down
4. throw out
5. put on

Activity 4

1. down
2. on
3. out
4. on
5. down to
6. on

Activity 5

1. threw out
2. get down
3. threw out
4. Putting on
5. get down

LESSON 10
COME OVER; HANG OUT; MOVE IN

ACTIVITY 1: CONVERSATION PRACTICE

A woman invites her friend to her house for dinner.

Read this conversation. Think about the meanings of the **3 new bold verbs**. Remember the meanings of the <u>underlined verbs</u> from earlier lessons. Then answer the comprehension questions.

Brooke: Hey, Karen, I'd like to invite you to **come over** for dinner on Saturday night.
Karen: Oh, thank you. I'd love to. Is it a special occasion?
Brooke: Not really. We haven't seen each other in a while. I was thinking we could just **hang out** after dinner, but we could also start watching the new season of that sci-fi TV show you like.
Karen: Oh, I'd love that! Thank you!
Brooke: Great! I'm looking forward to this. I haven't had anyone over to my new place since I **moved in.** It'll be a great chance to <u>bring out</u> the special tablecloth that was my grandmother's. I wasn't able to have people over when I had roommates and was living in that small apartment.
Karen: I can't wait to see your new place.
Brooke: It's great! I'm so much happier to be living alone.
Karen: I understand completely. I don't miss having roommates.
Brooke: I'll <u>go through</u> my cookbooks tonight, but I think I might make my mom's famous lasagna. Is that okay?
Karen: Is it vegetarian?
Brooke: Oh, that's right. You don't eat meat. Well, that's no problem—I can easily make it without meat.

Karen: That sounds delicious. What can I bring?
Brooke: How about something for dessert? I'll make a simple salad and get some bread and wine, and then we should be all set.
Karen: Oh, I haven't baked in a long time, but it might be fun to do that. I'll try to make something, but I also may <u>wind up</u> buying something.
Brooke: Either is okay with me.
Karen: What time should I <u>turn up?</u>
Brooke: Let's say 6:00. Oh, Karen, I have to <u>hang up</u> now—someone is at my door.
Karen: Six is good. See you Saturday!

1. What is happening on Saturday night?

    a. Karen is cooking for Brooke and her mother.
    b. Karen is going to Brooke's for dinner.
    c. Karen is moving to a new apartment.

2. Which of these statements is true about Brooke?

    a. She lives by herself.
    b. She likes her roommates.
    c. She works until 6:00.

3. Which of these statements is true about Karen?

    a. She lives by herself.
    b. She likes her roommates.
    c. She works until 6:00.

4. Where did Brooke learn how to make lasagna?

   a. from the internet
   b. from a cookbook
   c. from her mother

5. What will Brooke make for dinner?

   a. fresh bread and cheese
   b. a vegetarian dish
   c. We don't know from this conversation.

6. Who is bringing the dessert?

   a. Karen
   b. Brooke
   c. Brooke's mother

∼

ACTIVITY 2: LEARNING NEW PHRASAL VERBS

Read this information about 3 phrasal verbs. Study the example sentences carefully. To help learn them, read the example sentences aloud or write them on a sheet of paper or in a document.

#88: COME OVER

88: go to a place, usually where the speaker is

- Marcos, can you **come over** now?
- Do you want to **come over** to watch a movie?

#89: HANG OUT

89: be together with a certain person or people or be at a certain place

- I like to **hang out** at coffee shops.
- When I was a kid, I used to **hang out** at the tennis courts when my parents played. That's how I learned to play tennis!

#90: MOVE IN

90: settle into a new place

- When did you **move in**? How long ago was it?
- How long did you know Alex before you **moved in** with him?

ACTIVITY 3: PRACTICING IMPORTANT PHRASES

Give the phrasal verb for the meaning. Be sure to use the correct verb tense.

1. Don't arrive at the party before noon = Don't _____ _____ at the party before noon

2. begin to live with Anna and Romina = ____ ____ with Anna and Romina
3. spend time at my cousin's place = ____ ____ at my cousin's place
4. Can you arrive around 8? = Can you ____ ____ around 8?
5. spend a few hours with your friends = ____ ____ with your friends

∼

ACTIVITY 4: USING CORRECT PREPOSITIONS

Read the sentences carefully and add the missing prepositions for each phrasal verb.

1. Deciding to **move** ____ with someone is a big decision.
2. After school, they like to **hang** ____ at the arcade.
3. Would you like to **come** ____ for dinner on Saturday?
4. We ordered pizza for everyone after they helped us **move** ____ to our apartment.
5. We asked them to **come** ____ to our house to watch the championship game.
6. Teenagers spend a lot of time **hanging** ____ and playing video games.

∼

ACTIVITY 5: VERBS IN CONTEXT

Use the context to select the correct verb for the sentence.

1. (Come over, Hang out, Move in) and see my new furniture. It's beautiful!
2. We were able to (come over, hang out, move in) just an hour after signing the lease.
3. Are you (coming over, hanging out, moving in) for Game Night tonight?
4. I love (coming over, hanging out, moving in) with you.
5. We are so glad you (came over, hung out, moved in) next door to us!

ACTIVITY 6: ONLINE PRACTICE

You can practice the phrasal verbs from this lesson at

http://tinyurl.com/2b3r5kvy

Here you can use *Flashcards*, *Learn*, or *Match*. You can also have more guided practice with *Q-Chat*, which offers *Teach me*, *Quiz me*, and *Apply my knowledge*.

Answers for Lesson 10

Activity 1

1. b
2. a
3. a
4. c
5. b
6. a

Activity 3

1. come over
2. move in
3. hang out
4. come over
5. hang out

Activity 4

1. in
2. out
3. over
4. in
5. over
6. out

Activity 5

1. Come over
2. move in
3. coming over
4. hanging out
5. moved in

ABOUT THE PUBLISHER

Thank you for your time and attention! If you found the book useful, we hope you will leave a short review on the site where you purchased this book to let other readers know of your experience.

To be notified about new titles and special contests, events, and sales from Wayzgoose Press, please visit our website at

http://wayzgoosepress.com

and sign up for our mailing list. (We send email infrequently, and you can unsubscribe at any time.)

www.ingramcontent.com/pod-product-compliance
Lightning Source LLC
Chambersburg PA
CBHW060816050426
42449CB00008B/1682